Born in the Wrong Desert

poems by

Misha Tentser

MOUTHFEEL PRESS

Grateful acknowledgements to the following publications:
"For Mom" previously published with *Crosswinds Poetry Journal*.
"7 p.m. in Kyiv" previously published with *Terrain.org*.

Born in the Wrong Desert
Copyright © Misha Tentser, 2023

All rights reserved. No part of this book may be reproduced in print, digital, or recorded without written permission from the publisher or author.

Mouthfeel Press is an indie press publishing works in English and Spanish by new and established poets. We publish poetry, fiction, and non-fiction. Our print books are available through our independent bookstores, website, Bookshop.org, and other online and independent booksellers, or at author's readings. Ebooks are available through KOBO.

Cover Art by Octavio Quintanilla
Art Title: Frontextos, Los dias oscuros 234
Cover Design: Karen Dreher

Contact Information:
Mouthfeelbooks.com
Info.mouthfeelbooks@gmail.com

Print ISBN: 978-1-957840-06-2
Ebook ISBN: 978-1-957840-07-9

Published in the United States, 2023
First Printing in English
$12

TABLE OF CONTENTS

Fort Lowell and Columbus	*1*
Rincon Market Constellation	*2*
Dear Boris	*3*
Grant and Alvernon Burger King	*4*
Grant and Alvernon Love Story	*5*
Tall Tales at Benny's	*6*
Congregation Chaverim	*7*
After Burning Weeds in Peter Howell Neighborhood	*8*
Born in the Wrong Desert	*9*
Jesus Is Alive in Marta and Eduardo's Yard	*10*
Caravan Goods	*11*
Danny's Babo	*13*
Stoner Avenue	*14*
Fox Avenue	*16*
Go-Go Hair Salon	*17*
For Mom	*18*
7 p.m in Kyiv	*19*
Author's Biography	*25*

For Hayley Elizabeth Hall

Fort Lowell and Columbus

I can hear mom's violin
and dad's piano resonating
through the apartment,
Russian cartoons booming
on the T.V. in the kitchen,
and soup, somehow always soup,
simmering on the single-burner
stovetop. I wish I could hear
myself think in this house
of sound, where no one knows
silence or stillness or processed
food. I miss Carter's house
at Speedway and Wilmot,
with its clean, quiet walls
and fridge full of Lunchables—
a quiet food for a quiet boy
who shows me his room
of penguin stuffed animals,
which is how I feel next
to Carter, like a creature
from a faraway land plopped
into this desert, uneasy around
silence, searching for stillness
in hand-me-down noise.

Rincon Market Constellation

A.   B.
                                                                    E.

G.
                        C.   D.

                                       F.   H.

A. Boris, the fishmonger, butchers a salmon while we browse for wine. You yelp as he detaches the fish's head and smacks it down on the cutting board.
B. You pick a biodynamic red wine. The back of the label says the vintner uses endangered varietals indigenous to Northern Italy. Later, we decide the wine tastes like feet so we use it to make coq au vin. We pair the chicken with cold beer.
C. I order two cappuccinos at the counter.
D. The barista mispronounces my name. She scoffs when you correct her. I know how badly you want to climb over the counter and give her a stern talking to.
E. I pull on your sleeve and guide you to a table by the window. The soft light tempers the sharp edges of your expression. You look like the subject of a Vermeer.
F. We sneak a cigarette on the loading dock before I walk you to your parents' house.
G. A new employee cowers behind the seafood counter as Boris berates her for not descaling properly. His eyebrows are two angry caterpillars. I feel guilty for eavesdropping.
H. I sit with you and your parents on the patio. Your father is losing his hearing but refuses to wear a hearing aid. You think he doesn't want to listen to your mother anymore. I think he likes the peace and quiet. We sip our beers and stare across 6th Street.

Dear Boris

When I was 7, you yelled at me for smearing
your glass display with my grubby digits.
For a year, I had a recurring dream in which you
chased me around the market with your knife.
Every time, I hid behind the baguettes
and held my breath until your footsteps faded.
My mother used to call you a demigod
with hands the size of ruby red trout.
When she approached the counter,
your voice melted into a gentle tenor
as you waxed on about your days in Irkutsk.
After Rincon Market closed, my neighbor told me
you moved to Alaska to become a fisherman,
so I imagined you casting your line in a stream
the same color as the cloudless arctic sky,
wondering why you never said goodbye.

Grant and Alvernon Burger King

I have seen a different naked man
experiencing psychosis at Burger King
on three separate instances,
each time more troubling than the last,
pink and screaming and helpless
like a newly-hatched chick.

My psychiatrist friend tells me
there is a concentration of rehabs
in the vicinity, so Burger King Corporate
installed shotguns beneath the tills
to deter psychotic individuals,
but they don't have any bullets
and are meant more for intimidation.

I crumple at the cruelty required
to point a gun at someone
experiencing a psychotic break.
In this state, is a banana more a gun
than a shotgun is a gun?

In this state, is it easier
to purchase a banana or a gun?

Grant and Alvernon Love Story

I sit in Maria Cooper Library after our argument, one stubbed toe away from an emotional dumpster fire. A man in a button-up views pornography on a public desktop and the librarian pretends not to notice. I select a book about tornadoes from the reference section. I learn that in order for a tornado to be classified as a tornado, it must be in contact with both the earth and the base of a cloud.

Isn't it true that in order for me to love you, I must be in contact with both your earthly and cloud-based forms? I must be one with the physical confines of your being and the parts of you that float in the heavens. Your mind certainly floats in the heavens. You're always reimagining plots of classic films and wondering what animals you could take in a fight, like probably an armadillo but definitely not an angry goose.

I place the book back on the shelf and think of all the times we sat back to back on the carpet in our small living room reading about animals, or food, or weather patterns. I walk out of the library and catch the bus to Grant and Alvernon. A woman on the bus screams about George Bush. I meet you at Church's Chicken and we split a bucket. We apologize at the same time: you for breaking my favorite mug and me for overreacting.

I tell you about the tornadoes. You tell me you saw one once in Kansas. It was a few miles away but you felt its primal power. We get home and cuddle up on the couch. We watch the Vasyukov documentary about people living in the Russian taiga. A man builds a set of skis out of wood. Another man builds a hunting lodge in the forest. I wonder if they are happy the way we are happy.

Tall Tales at Benny's

I sit and inhale the steam of huevos rancheros, my afternoon aromatherapy placed in front of me by Sofia, one of the proprietors of Benny's on Grant and Treat and a close family friend. Sofia glides from table to table in her Skechers, slinging salsa refills and chatting up the regulars until she gets to my table, frowns, and asks why my hair *looks like a shag carpet*. So I scarf down the crispy corn tortillas smothered in roasted tomatoes and spicy green chiles, and run across Grant in midafternoon heat to Jesus' hole-in-the-wall barbershop, which is really just a long hallway adorned with vintage straight-razors and magic posters.

I slide into one of the two barber chairs. Jesus asks *what will it be today* as though I have been coming to see him for 30 years. Although I am tempted to say the usual, I ask him for a tight fade and beard trim, no straight-razor. Jesus buzzes the side of my head with a rusty Wahl. He tells me about the history of the building, which at one time was both a bar and a magic shop until the magic shop flopped and the bar lost its license. He tells me he bought the building in cash from a cowboy who signed the papers with a fountain pen and rode off on a speckled horse, never to be seen in this town again. It's at this moment I realize: Jesus is the purest incarnation of Tucson, steeped in tall tales and too much pomade, a marker of the wrinkles in time that stretch across my home.

I pay Jesus, stride out onto Grant, and spot a smoke shop advertising CBD gummies and other such elixirs. At the counter, I ask for a pack of Pall Malls and an orange soda. The cashier compliments my fade and I tell her it's Jesus' work. She responds with a warning to *never trust a word that guy ever says*. I thank her and stride out onto Grant. Cars zip past. I take the long way home.

Congregation Chaverim

At the bar mitzvah, Rabbi twerks
like there's no tomorrow. He shakes
his ass on the dance floor like OJ
with pulp as the mothers' eyes bulge
out of their prim and proper heads.

At 5th Street Deli, he smacks
on a bowl of matzoh ball soup,
ravenous and scarcely removed
from the hubbub of the city street.
The soup's heat fogs his acetate frames.
He is at home in this simple rapture.

At Saturday service, his palms
are to the sky when he asks
if we think bugs *go on hikes
to see waterfalls* and if sobriety
is an exercise in self-flagellation.
Would denial be the whip?
Would the body be a canvas?

At mom's Sukkot dinner, he winks
at me from across the table
like we share a secret. As I retire
to the porch to smoke, he follows
me outside, lights a small cigar,
and holds the flame to my cigarette.
We revel in stillness and vapor.

After Burning Weeds in Peter Howell Neighborhood

Rabbi says *silence is a fence around wisdom.*

The wind chimes on the back porch sing
for the first crisp day of Fall.

I have known peace like this in Tel Aviv,
sneaking a cigarette in my uncle's bathroom

while my family slumbers and the city roars
through the propped open window.

I have known peace like this in synagogues,
in the rustling before Yom Kippur service,

when mothers slip their children apple slices
to keep their stomachs from growling.

I have never spoken the language of stillness.
I drag a stick through the neighborhood wash.

I have never spoken the language of stillness.
Bicyclists zip along the 3rd Street bike path.

My Talmud's dog-eared pages turn in the breeze.

Born in the Wrong Desert

When Rabbi tells me
I'm a lost Jew born
in the wrong desert,
I feel my insides twist
toward Jerusalem,
flocks of worshippers,
shawarma spinning
in limestone alleys.

When I ask him why,
when I close my eyes
at Grande and Sonora,
I feel whole in the scent
of flour tortillas slapped
on the hot flat top,
he has no answer.

Jesus Is Alive in Marta and Eduardo's Yard

The bats have long flown south for winter.
My neighbors are grilling corn, so I bring

over a plate of latkes and salmon. They offer
me bass skin chicharrones. A man smoking

a cigar fixes me a plate. He asks if I have heard
the message of Jesus. I tell him I taste Jesus

in these elotes and charro beans. He shakes
his head and I grab a beer. Marta burrows

her nose into Eduardo's clavicle. Eduardo wraps
his hand around Marta's hip. The moon blooms

over the horizon. Guests disperse but I linger
in the yard. Eduardo busts out the mezcal

and pours each of us a nip. He chuckles
as my eyes water. I am warm, whole, still.

Caravan Goods

My friend Muhammad, the owner of Caravan Goods on Glean Street, knows my name means little bear in Russian so he slips a few pieces of honey candy into my bag. I know he prays five times a day and doesn't carry any pork products so I greet him with a warm salaam. The first time I walked into his shop by accident four years ago, the smell of spices overwhelmed me. I sneezed until tears trickled down my cheeks. Not to worry, he told me, many of your people have this reaction the first time.

Two years ago, Muhammad's sister found out she had late-stage breast cancer on her thirty-fifth birthday. He explained to me the shop would be closed for the week so he could visit her and say goodbye. When he came back, he looked older. His grief cast a shadow over his usually cheerful store. For a time, his regulars stopped coming because they couldn't bear to see him so devoid of joy. Eventually, the color returned to his face. Business picked up and he began chatting me up again, this time with the urgency of someone unsure of how much time he had left. I learned he was allergic to garlic, obsessed with Formula 1 racing, and longed to backpack through Europe. You're a good listener, he once told me as he poured himself a cup of black tea and slipped honey candy into my bag. (Nobody in the history of the universe had called me a good listener before.)

When I moved to Chicago for a few years, Muhammad told me to expect a call from his beloved brother Farid. On my third night in the city, Farid invited me over for dinner at his place in Rogers Park. As he opened the door to his apartment, a familiar smell of spices bombarded my nose. This time I did not sneeze. Over dinner, Farid told me his brother talked about me on the phone all the time. He said Muhammad talked about his regulars like his closest friends and often knew the most intimate details of their lives. He knew who had money troubles and who ate banana ice cream when they were feeling sad. He knew who was having an affair and who drank six limonadas a day in the summer heat. Now, when I visit Tucson, I stop by Muhammad's shop on the way to my parents' house on Fox Avenue. There he sits with his cup of black tea, chatting me up, stacks of lavash like giant moons welcoming me home.

Danny's Babo

The solo bartender says
thanks for your patience,
unaware that for me,
time has congealed
like two-week-old
hot and sour soup.
I would gladly sit
here for 20 years
subsisting on liquor
until my liver failed
and the rest of my body
sunk into this bar stool.

Maybe, when I'm
on my deathbed
I'll ask her nicely
to burn my body,
save my skull,
so she can mount
it on the wall.

Stoner Avenue

The green sign is still there.
I see it from my parents' porch.
I bet you 20 bucks it's the same one
you stole on a summer night in 2009
and re-attached before dawn.
I stood guard as you snuck up
with my dad's monkey wrench,
wearing my black Cubs hoodie,
a set of ridiculous sunglasses.
Do you remember how you tried
to slide it casually into your pants
and wound up cutting your leg,
leaving a faint trail of blood
leading back to the house?
You made me take your photo
with a joint in your mouth,
holding the sign like a prize fish
and wincing from the wound.
Did I make you re-attach the sign?
I was definitely concerned
that folks in the cul-de-sac
wouldn't know how to get home.
I wish you were home with me now.
There are so many other signs
I want to steal and re-attach with you,
like Hash Knife Circle or Tarantula Trail
or Manlove Street or Nirvana Place.
That last one would be your favorite.
I bet you wouldn't be able to let it go.
You dressed up as Kurt Cobain
for at least 4 Halloweens in a row.
I can't believe you only made it to 26.
You would've hated your funeral.

Your mother hired a string quartet
and some priest read a Bible passage.
I was sure we'd be sitting on my porch
talking about how pot is too strong
for any reasonable person these days,
and isn't it crazy that I can't remember
a single book we read in English class
but I remember which one of your ears
I pierced in my parents' backyard?
It was definitely the left one.
Your right one had a freckle on it.

Fox Avenue

My parents tell me they settled
in Arizona because they thought
all of America was the same.

Tucson was just like New York
but with roadrunners scurrying
down paved streets because God
forbid the streets are unpaved
in this cul-de-sac'd American dream.

Now, they live on a street
named Fox, a cunning animal
in Slavic folklore known to be wiser
than the bear, which is the meaning
of my name. Yet I remember
neither the rules of the forest
nor the language of my mother.

Because as a son of refugees, I'm too busy
defacing memories of the motherland
with greasy fingers, leaving smudges
on old photographs before linking
those fingers in prayer for salvation
that the future might bring.

Go-Go Hair Salon on Speedway

The woman from Yazd with the smooth hands says she cuts my hair carefully because I remind her of her son, the quiet dentist who lives in Los Angeles and FaceTimes her twice a week, always for longer than twenty minutes, asking her how her day is going and how is her health and would she like to hear a funny story about his out of touch clientele who whiten their teeth and get their groceries delivered, but he still hasn't found a nice Persian girl to marry and isn't that sad, she says, so hard to find your people, she says, one day you'll find a sweet Ukrainian girl, she says, especially with hair like this, all thick and wavy and chestnut, which reminds her of the chestnut trees in northern Iran, so abundant, weighed down branches spilling chestnuts onto the ground every fall, which the children gather and pelt each other with, and it's hard to tell children not to do something because that makes them want to do it more, which is why she doesn't tell her son to find a nice Persian girl, because he'll figure it out on his own, because he's a good man, like me, for listening to her talk for so long, and of course I tip her handsomely, and of course I promise to come back in six weeks, and of course she tells me her heart is with my Ukrainian family, and love will always triumph over war, so I push through the doors into the balmy spring afternoon and wonder why home is always so far away.

For Mom

Transfixed by monthly expenses, my mother
adds on the back of a piece of sheet music:
rotisserie chickens + beets + life insurance.

I wonder about her days in Moscow:
curly hair like an advertisement,
Levi's reeking of privilege.

The rocks thrown, the nights followed home,
it was the way the neighbor girl
looked at me as if I were an animal.

In her eyes I see the boy who never touched mitzvah,
who tattooed his body with unkosher creatures,
who pledged love to shiksas and ham sandwiches.

Yet I taste her love in peeled persimmons,
cinnamon dusted espresso,
kotletki slapped on the hot pan.

So I dust off my kippa
and sit before the Sukkot table,
reptilian brain lunging for dumplings.

Her gaze meets mine and I gulp.
A smile takes residence on her face
and her eyes gleam with tradition.

7 p.m. in Kyiv

It's Saturday morning. My mother and I sit on a bench at St. Philip's Plaza and sip our coffees. Cyclists walk their carbon fiber bicycles. Foothills matriarchs walk their freshly manicured dogs. It's been five days since my Ukrainian grandmother, my father's mother, told me over the phone that Russia has invaded Ukraine. Though my grandmother fled to Israel twenty years ago, my great uncle, her brother, stayed behind. From her I learned my great uncle has been trapped in Kyiv without cell or internet service since Tuesday. He and I usually speak on the phone once a month. Yesterday and today, I dialed his number a total of seventeen times. Every time I dial, I get an automated error message followed by the hiss of static. Sometimes, I swear I can hear the warmth of his voice within the static, so I stay on the line for a few minutes listening, wondering if he's trying to send me a secret message. It's like those ghost hunting TV shows where the host asks if there are any spirits in the dark living room of an abandoned house. Sometimes, the mic legitimately picks up a human-sounding voice. Other times, it's clear the "voice" is really just the sound of wind ripping through the old house. The viewer interprets the "voice" as human because they desperately want to believe in ghosts. I don't know if I believe in ghosts. I know I'm not ready to believe my great uncle is a ghost yet.

My mother tells me dictators start to lose their minds after twenty or so years in power. At that point, she says, they have little to no opposition and begin to experience intense paranoia, which forces them to make rash decisions, i.e., invade sovereign nations. She tells me state-controlled Russian media has been spouting propaganda regarding a Nazi-led genocide of ethnic Russians in Ukraine in an effort to garner support for the invasion amongst Russian citizens. The strategy seems to have worked. She tells me she has stopped using Russian Facebook because many of her friends and former classmates have been echoing the Russian media's propaganda and calling for the slaughter of so-called "Ukrainian neo-Nazis." This rhetoric makes her upset, she says, but she doesn't want to argue with them over the internet because it's exhausting, and she simply doesn't have the time. I tell my mother I haven't been paying attention to the news, which is a lie. I have seen the images of orphaned children and animals. I have read the reports of African students studying medicine in Ukraine experiencing overt racism at the Ukraine/Poland border as they try to flee, subject to a "hierarchy" of Ukrainian women first, then Ukrainian children, then Ukrainian men, then Africans. I have listened to reports from Radio Free Europe about journalists fleeing Russia after receiving death threats alongside photographs of their children walking to school.

I cry at the images. I cry at the reports. I cry at the broadcasts. But I don't cry in front of my mother. To her, I am the good son who walks the dog and helps her make soup. I am not the son who hasn't showered for four days, following news updates obsessively, refreshing Reddit every 15 minutes, knots in my throat leading down my back, too anxious to sleep, too inarticulate to express my feelings to those who care about me most.

My mother says she doesn't blame me for not watching the news. She says she has always believed ignorance to be bliss. She gestures in front of us. Look at all of these people in the plaza, she says. They are wealthy, dining in restaurants without masks, cracking jokes with one another, unaffected beyond the mild annoyance of higher gas prices. I think of the table I served last night at the restaurant I work at. I never tell guests my name unless they ask. These people asked. When I told them, they asked if I was Ukrainian. Too exhausted to lie, I told them I was. They smirked and told me they wouldn't be ordering Russian vodka from me in solidarity with "the Ukraine." Their faces were greasy and smug. I quickly turned to walk away from the table before I slapped every single one of those sunburnt, polo shirt-wearing assholes. I told my coworker

I was taking a break and stepped outside to center myself. When I came back in, I asked my coworker to take over the table. This is another thing I don't tell my mother.

My mother asks if I have completed any poems recently. At first, I tell her no, I have been too busy with work to write and I haven't felt particularly inspired. She says surely I've completed something; I haven't shared anything with her in months. I crack immediately. I tell her I've been working on a poem about Ukraine but it's a draft and I don't want to read it. She says I don't have to read it but she would like to see it anyway. I agree. I pull up the poem on my phone.

For My Homeland in Wartime

*Over the phone, my grandmother says "Russia
has invaded Ukraine" and I feel my heart rip*

*as it pulls towards a homeland built
out of my father's childhood memories.*

*When they tear us apart, will his memories
break into pieces or be swallowed by the sea?*

*On my way to work, I cry in the car
for my great uncle trapped in Kyiv,*

*bracing himself as tanks advance,
crushing orchids into chestnut soil.*

*When they tear us apart, will the birch trees
lining my grandfather's grave in Kyiv still sway?*

*Over coffee, my father says "we've lived through
worse" and I wonder how to take inventory*

of our bodies, splintered across continents,
eager to be made whole in an unfamiliar land.

When they tear us apart, will they bury
us in Odesa so we can taste the sea?

My mother holds my phone gingerly and reads the poem quietly to herself while I bite my nails. Her mouth forms into one taut line. I look out at the plaza. A wide brim hatted woman is too busy talking on her phone to realize her golden retriever is taking a piss in the fountain. A table of college kids clink flutes of sparkling wine on one of the restaurant's patios while a server tries to take their order. A leathery-looking man in a salmon polo ashes his cigar onto a patch of grass. I look back at my mother and see her take off her sunglasses and wipe her eyes.

I ask her if she likes the poem. She tells me she does, puts her sunglasses back on, and changes the subject. Maybe she's afraid to be vulnerable. She asks me if I have heard from my great uncle. I tell her no, that I haven't, that I have begun to worry if he is safe. She assures me he is just taking cover in the bomb shelter of his building, which he outfitted with cots, canned food, and even a television. I ask her how she knows this. She tells me that's the kind of person he is, a stubborn survivalist prepared for any situation. I tell her I am worried because I don't have any survivalist training. All of my skills are impractical: remembering customers' faces, chugging sparkling water without burping, identifying watch brands in movies.

"I would be useless if a world war broke out," I tell her.

"Just be grateful you don't live in Russia. You know men ages 18-60 are required to fight for Putin," she reminds me.

"If I had to fight for Putin, I would desert immediately."

"Why's that?"
"I would rather be executed than slaughter innocent civilians."
"What about your family? How would they feel about your execution?"
"At least I would die a noble death."
"Don't forget you are Russian and Ukrainian."
I take a beat.
"Why do you bring it up?"
"Because right now you are torn down the middle, like in your poem."

The dam breaks. I start crying in the middle of St. Philip's Plaza, keenly aware of the pissing dogs, the brunching boomers, and the college kids all staring at me. It's an absurdist nightmare. How can all of these people live as if the world isn't on the verge of collapse? All I want is for the earth to open up and swallow me whole. My mother touches my shoulder. I breathe and center myself. I tell her I feel like one half of my heritage is massacring the other half. I tell her she and my father are hardier people for having fled the Soviet Union, landing on their feet in the United States after so many years of struggling. I tell her I am too sensitive, too soft, too American. I tell her I don't know what to do or how to cope.

"That's one of the reasons why we make art," she tells me.

I agree and we fall silent.

My mother tells me she has to get going but to call her if I need anything. I walk her to her car. We hug and she tells me to keep my head up. As soon as she drives off, I dial my great uncle's number. As the line rings, I walk over to the bike path. It's 7 p.m. in Kyiv. Cyclists zip past me as I lean against the iron guard rail separating the path from the dry ravine. This time, instead of the error message and static, I get patched through to an automated voicemail asking me in Ukrainian to leave a message at the tone. I feel my palms start to sweat. I have to say something. What if this is the last message he will hear? The line beeps. I start speaking in rusty Russian, apologizing for not calling as often as I should, letting him know his family is thinking of him, and praying for a reunion. I realize I am speaking in the language of the soldiers destroying his homeland, the language deemed "superior" by the Soviet Union, the language my parents taught me instead of Ukrainian. The line beeps, indicating my voicemail has been recorded. I stay on the line listening to the warm hiss of static.

AUTHOR'S BIOGRAPHY

Misha Tentser is a Ukrainian-American Jewish poet based in Syracuse, where he is an MFA Candidate in Creative Writing at Syracuse University. His poetry has appeared in Back Patio Press *and Crosswinds Poetry Journal*. His creative nonfiction has been published with *Terrain.org*. When he is not writing, Misha is probably singing the praises of his hometown of Tucson, Arizona.